IR

Sports Illustrated KIDS

PLAY LIKE THE PROS

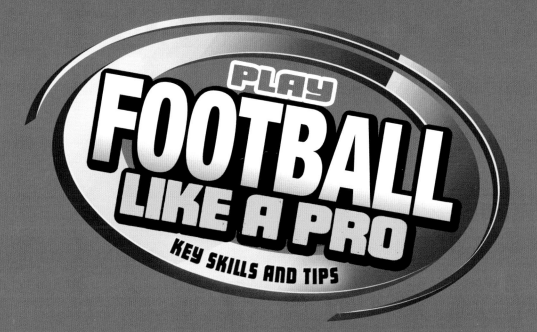

PLAY FOOTBALL LIKE A PRO
KEY SKILLS AND TIPS

BY MATT DOEDEN

Consultant:
Jeffrey L. Chambers
Head Athletic Trainer
Minnesota State University
Mankato, Minnesota

CAPSTONE PRESS
a capstone imprint

Books published by Capstone Press are manufactured with paper
containing at least 10 percent post-consumer waste.

Library of Congress Cataloging-in-Publication Data
Doeden, Matt.
    Play football like a pro: key skills and tips / By Matt Doeden.
    p. cm.—(Sports illustrated kids : play like the pros)
    Includes bibliographical references and index.
    Summary: "Provides instructional tips on how to improve one's
football skills, including quotes and advice from professional coaches
and athletes"—Provided by publisher.
    ISBN 978-1-4296-4825-7 (library binding)
    ISBN 978-1-4296-5646-7 (paperback)
1. Football—Training—Juvenile literature. I. Title. II. Series.
GV950.7.D63 2011
796.332071—dc22   2010007243

EDITORIAL CREDITS

Aaron Sautter and Anthony Wacholtz, editors; Ted Williams, designer;
    Eric Gohl, media researcher; Laura Manthe, production specialist

PHOTO CREDITS

Dreamstime/Lawrence Weslowski Jr., 27
Newscom, 28
Shutterstock/Denis Pepin, cover, 3 (football); kentoh, design element;
    Vjom, design element
Sports Illustrated/Al Tielemans, cover (right), 11, 16, 20 (all), 21, 22, 23;
    Bill Frakes, 6 (top), 13 (bottom), 25 (top); Bob Rosato, cover, (left),
    9 (top), 18, 24; Damian Strohmeyer, 4–5, 9 (bottom), 12, 19 (top), 26;
    John Biever, 7, 8, 10, 17, 19 (bottom); Peter Read Miller, 13 (top),
    25 (bottom); Simon Bruty, 6 (bottom), 14, 29

Printed in the United States of America in Stevens Point, Wisconsin.
122010   003019R

TABLE OF CONTENTS

TIPS ▼

▼ FEATURES

HIT THE GRIDIRON!

Millions of sports fans feel that nothing tops the excitement and drama of a National Football League (NFL) game. The clash between offense and defense makes football extremely popular. Fans love watching deep passes, long touchdown runs, and bone-crunching tackles.

Fans of all ages enjoy playing the game too. From local youth leagues to high school and college, players work hard to play football just like the professionals.

Do you dream of throwing passes like Peyton Manning or making crushing tackles like Ray Lewis? You may not yet have skills like the pros, but you can still work to improve your game. Keep reading for tips on how to improve your performance. With a lot of hard work and practice, you can learn to master any position on the field.

The snap from the center to the quarterback seems simple. But a botched snap can mean disaster. It ruins the play. Even worse, if the ball is fumbled, the team can lose possession of the ball. When playing quarterback, practice these steps to get the ball cleanly and keep the offense running smoothly.

PLACE YOUR HANDS CORRECTLY

Start by placing your hands below the center's rear. Your throwing hand should face palm down to receive the ball. Your other hand should face palm up, and your thumbs should be touching. Bend your elbows slightly to soften the force of the snap.

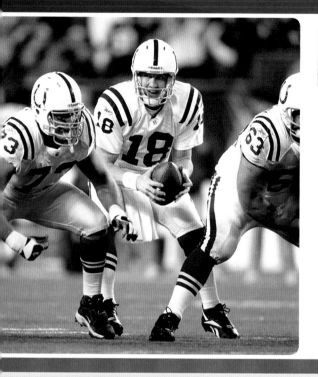

HANG ONTO THE BALL

When you shout out the signal, the center snaps the ball. The ball's laces should land directly on the palm of your throwing hand. Secure the ball, then drop back behind the center. With a clean snap, the play should be off to a good start.

When defenses are putting heavy pressure on the quarterback, offenses will sometimes use a formation called the shotgun. The shotgun gives the quarterback more time to find open receivers. The quarterback stands several yards behind the center. The center snaps the ball through the air to the quarterback. To receive the snap, the quarterback holds both hands out, usually with the tips of the thumbs touching.

▼ The Shotgun

↳ fumble—when a player drops the ball on the field

2 HOW TO COMPLETE A PASS

The quarterback's job is to make sure the offense runs smoothly. To do this, he has to get the ball to open receivers down the field. Practice these moves, and you'll soon be making successful passing plays on game day.

DROP BACK

After taking the snap, step back into the pocket. This is called a drop. The length of the planned pass affects the number of steps you take. Most drops are three, five, or seven steps. Taking more steps means it will take longer to complete the play. Longer plays give receivers more time to get open downfield.

↳ pocket—the protected area behind the offensive line between the two offensive tackles

FIND AN OPEN RECEIVER

From the pocket, look for an open receiver. Receivers are considered open if no defenders can get between them and a well-thrown pass. The defense is coming after you, so decide quickly where to throw the ball.

STEP INTO YOUR THROW

As you make your pass, shift your weight to the foot opposite your throwing arm. Stepping into the pass gives it more power, which helps the ball travel quickly. It can also help you launch a really deep pass downfield.

PASS THE BALL

It's time to throw the ball. Keep a firm grip with three or four fingers on the laces. Your non-throwing shoulder should be pointed at the target. Bring your throwing arm back, then swing it forward with the nose of the ball pointed toward the target. Release the ball about three-fourths of the way through your swing.

3 HOW TO HANG ONTO THE BALL

Keeping a good grip on the football is key for any ball carrier. This basic rule is true for quarterbacks, wide receivers, and tight ends. But it's especially true for running backs. A back's speed and power will be useless if he can't hold onto the ball. Fumbles can kill offensive drives and get running backs a seat on the bench.

HOLD ON TIGHT

The first step in carrying the football correctly is to place one point of the ball in your palm. Your wrist and arm should curve around the ball, forming a sort of cradle. Use this cradle to hold the ball tightly against your body. Place your other hand or arm in front of or on top of the ball for extra protection.

USE THE OUTSIDE ARM

Whether running left or right, the ball should be held in the arm nearest the sideline. The chances of a direct hit on the ball are much less if it's carried in the outside arm. If the ball does pop loose, there's a greater chance that it will bounce safely out-of-bounds.

"When there are people around you, sometimes you can fight for extra yards, but you've got to make sure you have [the football] close to your body with maybe two hands on it. You hate the feeling of when you fumble."
-LADAINIAN TOMLINSON, RUNNING BACK, NEW YORK JETS

Running backs dream of scoring on a big run. But big runs still start with the basics. Running backs must get the ball past the line of scrimmage before thinking about scoring. Follow these tips to burst through holes for big-time runs.

RECEIVE THE BALL

To receive a hand off, form a pocket with both arms and hands. The quarterback will thrust the ball into this pocket. Be sure to give the quarterback enough space between your hands to correctly place the football. Secure the ball with both hands. Then hold it against your body before heading toward the line of scrimmage.

↳ **line of scrimmage**—the imaginary line that separates the offense from the defense

FIND A HOLE

Next, look for a hole, or open running lane. Most running plays are designed to go to a specific hole. Head for that hole first. If the running lane is closed, keep looking for an opening. When you see a lane, go for it!

USE YOUR BLOCKERS

No player can do anything alone. Running backs rely on their blockers to help them get past the line of scrimmage. Watch the backs of your blockers to see the direction they're pushing the defenders. Cut behind the blockers in the opposite direction, then blast through the hole.

5 HOW TO RUN ROUTES

Successful passing plays depend on the quarterback knowing where his receivers will be. Receivers need to know the playbook so they can run accurate routes for any given play. Practice these basic routes and you'll soon be making some awesome catches.

● **FLAG/POST**

Run straight up the field, then angle toward the goal flag in the corner of the end zone. Another version of this route is to turn and run at an angle toward the goal post.

● **OUT**

Take a few steps forward, then quickly turn and run toward the sideline.

● **CURL**

Run straight down the field a set distance. Then quickly turn and come back toward the ball.

● **SLANT**

Run straight for about 5 yards. Then turn and run diagonally toward the middle of the field.

● **FLY**

Run straight up the field. Look back over your shoulder to watch for the ball.

Running a good route won't mean much if you don't catch the ball. The best receivers try to catch the ball with their hands, not their body. Practice the following steps to make amazing catches just like the pros.

CATCHING IT HIGH

Keep your hands up and together. Form a diamond shape with the tips of your thumbs and index fingers touching. This hand position creates a pocket for the ball. As the ball comes in, close your fingers around it to secure it.

CATCHING IT LOW

For a low pass, keep your hands down. Touch your pinkie fingers together and face your palms up to form a basket. To secure the ball, cradle it with your fingers and thumbs.

CATCHING IT OVER YOUR SHOULDER

To catch the ball while running downfield, reach your arms up toward the ball. Touch your pinkies like you would for a low pass. Face your palms up and toward the ball to pull it in. Be sure to always keep your eyes on the ball.

PULL IT IN

Once the catch is made, pull the ball toward your body to secure it as quickly as possible.

"Defensive backs are taught to ... tug your hands away from the football at all times. You have to have really strong hands to get the ball, and then you have to tuck it away really quickly."

HOW TO BLOCK ON THE LINE

Offensive linemen are the unsung heroes of football. They have one of the most important jobs during a game. It's up to them to keep defenders away from the ball carrier. As a lineman, you have two jobs. You must keep pass rushers away from the quarterback. And you need to open holes for the running back.

WORK ON YOUR STANCE

To block, you need a good, solid stance. The two main types of stances are the three-point and the four-point. For the three-point stance, stand with your knees bent, head up, and shoulders square. Keep one hand on the ground. For the four-point stance, place both hands on the ground.

Your stance should be comfortable and balanced. You should be able to quickly move left, right, forward, or backward, depending on the play.

OPEN A HOLE

Run blockers open up running lanes and protect the ball carrier. At the snap, surge forward. Drive your shoulder pads into the defender to move him backward or to one side. Don't grab his jersey or wrap your arms around him. Those moves can result in costly holding penalties.

PROTECT THE PASSER

For passing plays, you want to keep defenders from getting to the quarterback. At the snap, drop back into a blocking stance with your feet apart and hands forward. Use your hands and shoulders to push defenders away from the passer.

Linemen use some trickery for screen passes. They often let defenders get past them, pretending to get beat on the play. Once the defenders run by the linemen, the quarterback flips the ball to a running back or receiver. The offensive linemen then run up the field to block for the ball carrier.

The Screen Pass

HOW TO MAKE A GREAT TACKLE

Good defense begins and ends with solid tackling. Good form and position help you stuff the ball carrier. Work on these tips to keep players from breaking free and scoring on a big play.

KEEP YOUR HEAD UP

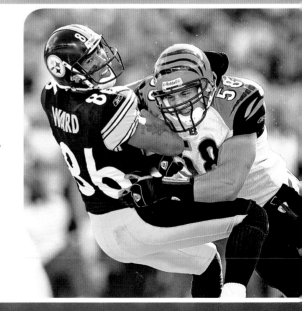

To make a tackle, meet the ball carrier with your knees bent, shoulders square, and head up. Keeping your head up helps you see where to hit your opponent. It also helps prevent injuries.

WRAP UP YOUR OPPONENT

Step into the ball carrier, placing your shoulder into his chest. Bring your arms up and around your opponent to "wrap him up." Push off the ground with your legs to drive the ball carrier backward and toward the ground.

USE YOUR BODY

If you use good form, the ball carrier will have a hard time escaping a tackle. However, it isn't always possible to be in position to make a perfect tackle. Be ready to use your body in any way necessary to legally bring your opponent to the ground.

9 HOW TO RUSH THE PASSER

Nothing throws a quarterback off his game more than a good pass rush. As a defensive lineman, you must find a way around the blockers to get to the quarterback. You can use one or more of the following moves to do this. Try mixing up your moves so the offense won't know what's coming.

SPEED RUSH

Line up on the outside of the offensive tackle to start a speed rush. As soon as the ball is snapped, take a big step toward the side of the blocker. Swing your arms into the blocker and roll past him. If everything goes right, you'll be on your way to the quarterback.

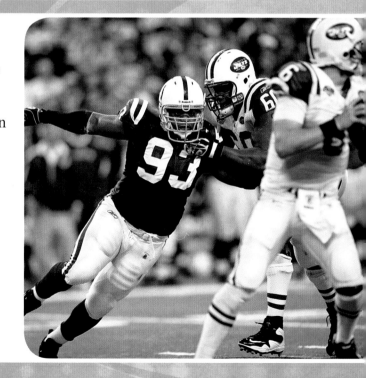

HAND RUSH

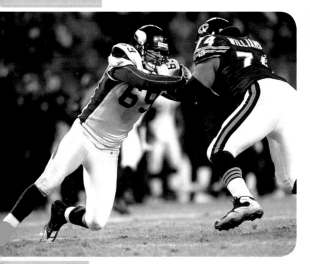

At the snap, quickly shoot out one or both hands into the blocker's chest. Try to force the blocker to open up, or turn, his stance. If he does, you can rush past him and try to sack the quarterback.

HUMP RUSH

This power rush starts the same way as a speed rush. But instead of rolling around the blocker, use your arms and power to push him out of the way. If you can throw him off balance, you'll have a free shot at the quarterback.

Sometimes defenses use a blitz to send extra players to rush the quarterback. The blitz works because the offense doesn't have enough men to block all of the pass rushers. But a blitz can be risky because there are fewer players left to cover downfield. A quick-thinking quarterback can throw the ball quickly to an open receiver during a blitz.

The Blitz

↳ sack— when a defensive player tackles the quarterback behind the line of scrimmage

HOW TO COVER A RECEIVER

Defensive backs may have the most demanding jobs on the field. Cornerbacks and safeties must chase receivers all over the field. They're also the last line of defense against a running back who has broken through the defensive line for a big play.

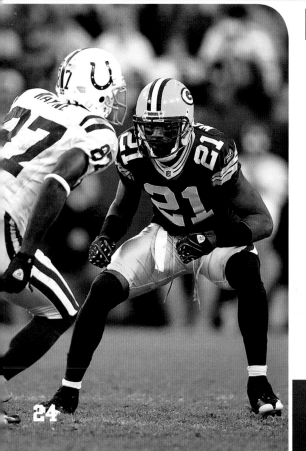

KNOW YOUR ROLE

Playing defense in the secondary depends on the position you're playing. Safeties need to figure out the play and be ready to react to it. They need to be ready to come forward for a run or drop back for a pass. Cornerbacks must backpedal as the receivers come off the line. They must figure out a receiver's route and run with the receiver.

COVER THE OPPONENT

In a man-to-man defense, defensive backs each match up with a receiver. You want to stay close to the receiver to make a play on the ball. In a zone defense, each defender covers an area on the field. Try to keep receivers in front of you so they can't gain big yardage.

MAKE THE PLAY

When the ball is thrown, your first job is to knock it down. Make sure the receiver doesn't get his hands on it. However, don't reach out and grab the receiver. If you do, you risk a costly interference penalty. Sometimes you may be in a position to intercept the ball. For an interception, use the same methods receivers use to catch the ball.

↳ **secondary**—the group of defensive players who line up behind the linebackers

↳ **intercept**—to catch a pass made by the opposing quarterback

HOW TO PLACEKICK

The kicking game is often overlooked in football. But it's critical to scoring points and winning games. With good form and plenty of practice, a kicker can be one of a team's best weapons.

PICK A STYLE

There are two ways to kick the ball—straight and soccer style. Straight kickers bring their foot straight up into the ball. However, soccer-style kicking is far more popular. Soccer-style kickers swing their leg at an angle to kick the ball. This style usually provides more power and better accuracy for the kick.

GET SET

A placekick starts with a long snap and a hold. The holder lines

up about seven yards behind the line of scrimmage. As the placekicker, you'll line up behind and to one side of the holder. Measure out two or three steps behind the holder to take as an approach.

LET IT FLY

The holder receives the snap and places the tip of the ball on the ground. He rotates the ball so the laces face away from you. Approach the ball and plant your non-kicking foot just in front of it. Then swing your kicking foot so it strikes the lower part of the ball. Be sure to follow through with your kicking leg to give your kick more power.

"I take it one kick at a time. I go into every kick with a clean slate, and whether I've made 20 in a row or whether I've missed two in a row, it doesn't matter. You've got to make the next one."
-RYAN LONGWELL, KICKER, MINNESOTA VIKINGS

HOW TO PUNT

Not all drives end in a score. Punting is an important part of gaining field position. Punters need to kick for distance and hang time. Practice these steps to make incredible, high-flying punts.

GET INTO YOUR STANCE

The first step is lining up and getting in a punting stance. In the NFL, punters usually line up about 15 yards behind the line. This position gives them room to kick and results in fewer blocked kicks. Set your feet about shoulder-width apart. Hold your hands forward with your elbows bent, so you're ready to receive the snap.

CATCH THE SNAP

Receive the snap with both hands. Use the hand matching your punting leg to line up the ball for your kick. Be sure the football's laces are facing away from your kicking foot.

MAKE THE KICK

Begin the kick by taking a half-step with your punting leg. Next, take a full step with the off leg. Finally, swing your punting leg up to meet the ball as you release it with your hands. Keep your eyes on the ball the whole time. After the ball is in the air, you become a defender. Run down the field and help tackle the punt returner.

It takes a lot of work and skill to make it in the NFL. The pros put in hundreds of hours of practice. They also make plenty of mistakes. But even the biggest stars had to start somewhere. It's never too late to get started. With a lot of hard work and practice, one day you may play football just like the pros!

GLOSSARY

BLITZ—a play in which extra defenders are sent to rush the quarterback

FUMBLE—when the ball carrier drops the ball while trying to advance it on the field

INTERCEPT—to catch a ball thrown by the opposing quarterback

LINE OF SCRIMMAGE—the imaginary line separating offense from defense; each play begins at the line of scrimmage

PENALTY—a punishment for breaking the rules; in football, penalties result in a loss of yardage for the offending team

POCKET—the protected area behind the offensive line

ROUTE—the path a receiver runs during a play

SACK—when a quarterback is tackled behind the line of scrimmage

SECONDARY—the group of defensive players who line up behind the linebackers; the secondary usually includes safeties and defensive backs

SHOTGUN—a formation in which the quarterback takes the snap from several yards behind the line of scrimmage

STANCE—the position of a player's feet and body

READ MORE

Gitlin, Marty. *Football Skills: How to Play Like a Pro.* How to Play Like a Pro. Berkeley Heights, N.J.: Enslow Publishers, 2009.

Jacobs, Greg. *The Everything Kids' Football Book: The All-Time Greats, Legendary Teams, Today's Superstars—And Tips On Playing Like A Pro.* Cincinnati, Ohio: Adams Media, 2010.

Wingate, Brian. *Football: Rules, Tips, Strategy, and Safety.* Sports from Coast to Coast. New York: Rosen Publishing Group, Inc., 2007.

INTERNET SITES

FactHound offers a safe, fun way to find Internet sites related to this book. All of the sites on FactHound have been researched by our staff.

Here's all you do:

Visit *www.facthound.com*

Type in this code: 9781429648257

INDEX ⅂